USBORNE

FIRST WORLD WAR

PICTURE BOOK

Struan Reid

Illustrated by Ian McNee

Designed by Tom Lalonde and Samantha Barrett

Edited by Jane Chisholm

Consultant: Victoria Kingston, Historian, Imperial War Museums

Contents

With thanks to Madeleine James

Published in association with Imperial War Museums

The First World War

The First World War broke out in 1914 and quickly engulfed all of Europe and beyond, with fighting on such a huge scale it was known as the 'Great War'. New weapons such as tanks and planes were used for the first time. By the end, in 1918, more than 16 million people had been killed.

1. The fuse is lit

On June 28, 1914, Archduke Franz Ferdinand, heir to the throne of Austria-Hungary, was shot dead in the Bosnian capital, Sarajevo, by an assassin recruited by a Serbian terrorist group. One month later, on July 28, Austria declared war on Serbia. Germany backed Austria and then declared war against Russia and France.

2. The Central Powers and Allies

The Germans marched into Belgium on August 4, 1914. Britain had signed a treaty to protect Belgium, and so declared war on Germany. Europe divided into two camps: the Central Powers: Germany and Austria-Hungary, and later Turkey and Bulgaria, and the Entente Powers or Allies: France, Russia, Britain, and later Italy and the USA.

Many people back home believed that the fighting would all be over by Christmas.

3. Gallipoli campaign

In April, 1915, the Allies set out to capture Gallipoli in Turkey and attack the capital, Constantinople. It was a disaster: after eight months they had to withdraw, with 44,000 soldiers dead, and about 110,000 evacuated because of disease.

4. The longest battle

The Battle of Verdun in France, fought between the French and Germans, lasted from February 21 to December 18, 1916. At least 260,000 soldiers were killed and half a million wounded. There was a huge number of casualties, but neither side was victorious.

By the end of the fighting, the medieval city of Verdun lay in ruins.

5. Fighting at sea

After two years of light skirmishes in the North Sea, the British and German navies finally confronted each other at the Battle of Jutland, Denmark, in 1916. It was the only major battle of the War to be fought at sea. By the end, 15 British and 11 German ships had been sunk, but there was no clear winner.

6. The Somme Offensive

On July 1, 1916, British and French troops advanced on German positions near the River Somme in northern France. But they were met by fierce resistance, and fighting continued until November 19. With nearly 1.5 million soldiers killed or wounded, it ended up as one of the bloodiest battles in history.

Fighting at the Somme

7. The USA joins the War

The USA declared war on Germany on April 6, 1917, after months of German provocation, and the first US forces landed in France on June 25, 1917.

The first US soldiers arrive in Europe.

8. Russia drops out

Following the abdication of Tsar Nicholas II a year earlier, on March 3, 1918, the new Russian Communist government signed the Treaty of Brest-Litovsk and withdrew from the War. This enabled the Germans to move extra forces to the Western Front and launch a new attack.

9. The tide turns

The Battle of Amiens began on August 8, 1918. Morale among German forces was now very low, and the Allies succeeded in pushing deep into German-held territory. This was a major turning point in the War and marked the beginning of a 95-day offensive that would lead to Allied victory.

The Signing of Peace in the Hall of Mirrors, Versailles, painted by William Orpen

10. The end of the War

On October 30, 1918, Turkey surrendered and on November 10 the German Kaiser went into exile in the Netherlands. At 11 o'clock on November 11, the eleventh month of 1918, Germany and the Allies signed the Armistice and there was a ceasefire. 37 million people – military and civilian – had been killed or wounded. On June 28, 1919, the Germans reluctantly signed the Treaty of Versailles, ending the War. Most considered the terms too severe: war would break out again 20 years later.

A call to arms

During the First World War, televisions hadn't been invented and few people owned radios. Governments used posters and magazines with powerful images to encourage men to join up, and to remind people that they were fighting for survival.

This poster, showing the face of Field Marshal Lord Kitchener, British Secretary of State for War, is one of the most famous of the entire War. He appeals directly to all the able-bodied men of Britain to enlist as soldiers.

"YOUR COUNTRY NEEDS **YOU**"

Kitchener organized the largest volunteer army that Britain had ever seen. More than 750,000 signed up in less than a month.

This Russian poster shows the German ruler, Kaiser Wilhelm, as a skeletal figure of Death, carrying a scythe to cut down the Russian soldiers. The message to the people back home is to support their army against the German killing machine.

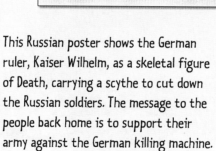

This striking German poster appeared in October 1918, just a month before the end of the War. It encourages people to subscribe to the 9th German war loan, to raise extra money for the war effort.

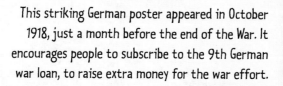

With the heading *U Boote Heraus!* ('The U-boats are out!'), this German poster of 1917 advertises the first submarine propaganda movie. The U-boat commander is peering through the submarine's periscope, while an enemy ship he has just attacked is sinking.

Submarines could stalk their prey for long distances, undetected. When the timing was right, the submarine commander issued the order to open fire.

I WANT YOU FOR U.S. ARMY

NEAREST RECRUITING STATION

Four million copies of this poster were printed between 1917 and 1918.

The USA entered the War in 1917 and immediately began a recruiting campaign. In this poster, a character called Uncle Sam is dressed in the stars and stripes of the US flag, and urges people to join up and fight.

WOMEN OF BRITAIN SAY — "GO!"

With more and more men being called up to fight, jobs on farms and in factories were taken by women. They performed a vital role, supplying food and equipment. They drove trains, served in the police and worked at coal mines. All this would change their position in society.

THESE WOMEN ARE DOING THEIR BIT

LEARN TO MAKE MUNITIONS

The British Women's Land Army kept the country fed. They tended animals, operated farm equipment, and harvested the crops.

The image of women guarding the nation's values was an important propaganda tool, helping to maintain morale at home and among the soldiers. With sad but brave faces, these women tell their menfolk to fight, while they will protect the family.

5

Fighter planes

The First World War was the first major conflict in which planes were used. The pilots who flew the fighter planes were some of the most dashing figures of the War.

British Bristol F.2B

The round symbol was placed on the top and bottom of the wings.

Larger and heavier than many other fighters, the Bristol was quick and agile in the air. With a high top speed, it could compete against smaller and lighter planes. Solid and reliable, a number of Bristols served in the British and Polish air forces well into the 1930s.

Firepower: 2 machine guns

Flight crew: 2

Top speed: 198kph (123mph)

This was the symbol displayed on the wings of planes of the British Royal Flying Corps, the original name for the Royal Air Force.

British Sopwith Pup

Firepower: 1 machine gun

Flight crew: 1

Top speed: 180kph (112mph)

The Pup first entered service in 1916 with the Royal Naval Air Service and Royal Flying Corps. Light and agile, it soon proved superior to German planes. Used on the Western Front and in defending Britain, in 1917 it was superseded by even better fighter planes, such as the Sopwith Camel.

Among the Pup's main targets were the lumbering Zeppelin airships that came to bomb London.

French Nieuport 11

Firepower: 1 machine gun

Flight crew: 1

Top speed: 156kph (97mph)

Wing symbol of the *Service Aéronautique*, the original name for the French Air Force.

Nicknamed *Bébé* (meaning 'Baby'), the small Nieuport was designed to compete in air races, but was adapted as a fighter plane during the War. Strong and fast, it soon outclassed its main enemy: the German Fokker.

German Fokker DVII

Firepower: 2 machine guns

Flight crew: 1

Top speed: 189kph (117mph)

Symbol of the Imperial German Air Force, or *Fliegertruppen*

Introduced in May 1918, the DVII was a late entry into the War. It had a simple but very strong design, making it fast and rugged, and it could climb and dive at steep angles, to avoid enemy fire.

French Spad S.XIII

The Spad was equipped with a powerful engine, which made it faster than most of its rivals. Strong and good in dives, it wasn't very agile in the air, which could make it an easy target. Despite this, it was very popular with its pilots.

Firepower: 2 machine guns

Flight crew: 1

Top speed: 218kph (135mph)

One of the War's most famous pilots, French air ace Georges Guynemer, helped to design the Spad.

Austrian Aviatik D.I

A solid fighter plane, with a good speed and large, comfortable cabin, the Aviatik was never popular with its pilots. Its engine had a tendency to overheat and its guns were mounted in an awkward position, making it vulnerable in the air.

Firepower: 2 machine guns

Flight crew: 1

Top speed: 185kph (115mph)

This symbol was also used by the Austro-Hungarian Air Force, or *Luftfahrtruppen*.

Bombers

Aerial bombardment was a terrifying new development that appeared early in the War. Cities such as London, far from the battlefront, were now exposed to attacks from the air.

French Breguet 14

Firepower: 2-3 machine guns

Flight crew: 2

Top speed: 175kph (109mph)

Bomb load: 300kgs (661lbs)

The Breguet 14 was one of the most lethally successful bombers of the War. Its frame of metal, rather than wood, and its simple, boxy design made it stronger, lighter and more agile than most other bombers.

Symbol displayed on the wings of French planes.

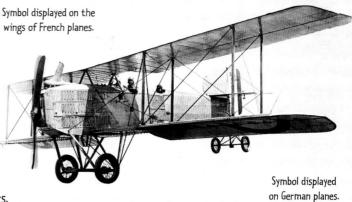

Symbol displayed on German planes.

German Zeppelin

Firepower: 5 machine guns

Flight crew: 15

Top speed: 136kph (85mph)

Bomb load: 2,000kgs (4,400lbs)

The Zeppelin was a rigid airship, first developed in the 1890s by German soldier and engineer Ferdinand von Zeppelin. The German navy used 115 of them to look out for enemy ships. Other Zeppelins were used for bombing raids on cities such as London and Paris.

British Handley Page Type 0

Firepower: 5 machine guns

Flight crew: 4-5

Top speed: 157kph (97mph)

Bomb load: 907kgs (2,000lbs)

When the Handley Page 0/100 first entered service in 1916, it was one of the largest planes ever built. A more powerful version replaced it in April 1918, the 0/400, designed to carry out bombing raids on German Zeppelin bases.

After the War, a number of Handley Pages were converted into 12-seat passenger planes, flying between London and Paris.

Symbol displayed on the wings of British planes.

German Gotha G.V

Firepower: 2-3 machine guns

Flight crew: 3

Top speed: 140kph (87mph)

Bomb load: up to 1,500kgs (3,307lbs)

The Gotha was Germany's most famous bomber. From 1917, it was used to replace the Zeppelins in bombing raids over London. But its engines weren't very powerful, and more Gothas were lost due to crash landings than to enemy fire.

British Airco DH.4

Firepower: 2-3 machine guns

Flight crew: 2

Top speed: 230kph (143mph)

Bomb load: 210kgs (463lbs)

In June 1923, two DH4s of the US Army Air Service performed the first mid-air refuel exercise.

Introduced in 1917, the DH.4 was easy to fly and reasonably fast, able to outperform many fighter planes. This made it very popular with pilots. It could also reach high altitudes, and was the first British bomber designed especially for daytime bombing raids.

Italian Caproni Ca.36

Firepower: 2 machine guns

Flight crew: 4

Top speed: 137kph (85mph)

Bomb load: up to 800kgs (1,760lbs)

A type of Ca.3 bomber, used by both the Italian army and navy, this was the first plane to carry out long-distance bombing missions. Ca.3s also flew in the British Royal Flying Corps, until they were replaced in 1918 by the Handley Page Type 0/400.

Symbol displayed on the wings of planes of the Italian Air Service, *Servizio Aeronautico*.

The rear gunner stood in a cage behind the wings, exposed to the freezing wind.

Tanks and guns

Tanks were used for the first time in battle in the First World War. Designed like mobile fortresses, their long metal tracks enabled them to move across deep trenches and thick mud.

British Mark I tank

Firepower: 2 main guns, 4 machine guns
Crew: 8
Top speed: 6kph (4mph)

The Mark I, which went into service in 1916, was the first tank of all. It was lozenge-shaped, with tracks that wrapped all the way around its two sides. But it was cumbersome and very slow and, as a result, not much use on the battlefield.

German A7V Panzer

Firepower: 1 main gun, 6 machine guns
Crew: 18
Top speed: 15kph (9mph)

Known as the 'moving fortress' because of its huge square shape, the A7V was the first German-built tank. Its two engines made it faster than the British Mark I, but its top-heavy design meant it often got stuck in mud.

The first tank-against-tank battle took place in April 1918, when three A7Vs surprised three British Mark IV tanks.

Two of the Mark IVs were outgunned by the A7Vs, but eventually the other Mark IV was able to force back the three German tanks.

Symbol displayed on German tanks.

French Char Renault tank

Firepower: 1 main gun, or 1 machine gun

Crew: 2

Top speed: 7kph (4mph)

Also known as the FT-17, this is considered to be the first modern tank. It had a fully rotating turret top, with an engine at the back and driver at the front. This layout is still used in tanks today.

Char Renaults were so successful that they were still being used by the French army as late as 1945.

British Mark A tank

Firepower: 4 machine guns

Crew: 3

Top speed: 13.4kph (8.3mph)

The Mark A, also known as the 'Whippet', first went into battle in the last months of the War. But it became the most successful British tank, inflicting huge damage on the enemy. It was fast and powered by two engines – one for each track.

In June 1918, the first identification stripes were used on a British tank – three stripes of white-red-white.

French Canon de 75 field gun

Maximum range: 6.9km (4.3 miles)

Operating crew: 6

Weight: 1.54 tonnes (1.5 tons)

Introduced in 1897, the 75 is regarded as the first modern field gun. The gun barrel could move back and forth during firing, while the wheels remained fixed. As it didn't need to be re-aimed after each shot, it increased the rate of fire.

German L/12 M-Gerät gun

Maximum range: 12.5km (7.7 miles)

Operating crew: 200

Weight: 43.7 tonnes (43 tons)

The huge L/12 had to be pulled around by tractors. Once in position, it took the crew more than six hours to get it ready for firing. Its great power earned it a reputation as a fortress-destroyer.

The L/12 was also known as 'Big Bertha', after Bertha Krupp, owner of the Krupp company that built it.

Army vehicles

Lots of vehicles were needed at the battlefront. Military cars could travel faster than tanks and inflict serious damage. Soldiers were transported in buses and trucks, while riders on motorcycles carried vital messages.

German Ehrhardt E-V/4

Firepower: 3 machine guns

Crew: 8-9

Top speed: 61.3kph (38mph)

Length: 5.3m (17ft, 4in)

E-V/4 cars first rolled off the production line in 1917 and were sent to strengthen German forces on the Eastern Front. With their tall, flat sides, the vehicles gave the soldiers inside a commanding view of their surroundings.

Symbol displayed on German vehicles.

At the end of the War, when Germany was rocked by revolution, E-V/4s were used to control riots in many German cities.

British B43 bus

Also known as: 'Ole Bill'

Carried: 25 fully-equipped troops

Top speed: 26kph (16mph)

Entered service: 1914

The B-Type bus was first used in 1914 as a passenger bus. During the War, 900 B-Types were used as troop carriers, and sometimes as ambulances or mobile pigeon lofts for communication services.

The buses were stripped down to make room for troops and their equipment.

British Austin

Firepower: 2 machine guns   **Top speed:** 60kph (37mph)
Crew: 4   **Length:** 4.9m (16ft)

Based on the chassis of an Austin car, this military vehicle had thick metal plating and solid rubber wheels for use on battlefields. Some were exported to Russia. From 1918, the Russians produced their own version: the Ostin-Putilov.

Italian Lancia IZ

Firepower: 3 machine guns

Crew: 6

Top speed: 60kph (37mph)

Length: 5.4m (17ft, 7in)

Markings displayed by the Italian army.

Introduced in 1916, the IZ was built by truck manufacturer Lancia, based on a truck design. It had a rotating double turret on its roof, armed with three guns.

This later model, the IZM, entered service in 1918. It was faster and equipped with a single turret and two machine guns.

British Gun carrier Mark 1

Gun carried: 60-pounder or howitzer

Crew: 4 + gun crew

Top speed: 6kph (4mph)

Engine: 105hp gasoline

Based on the Mark 1 tank, this was the first ever motorized gun carrier. The gun was on a ramp at the front, with the engine in a large steel box at the rear.

View of the gun carrier from the rear.

The gun was winched into an open space at the front.

British Douglas motorcycle

Produced in: Bristol, England   **Engine size:** 348cc
Carried: 1 driver

When the War broke out, the British army needed fast vehicles for dispatch riders carrying important messages between army units. The Douglas 2 was strong, fast and reliable, and good at scrambling over muddy battlefields.

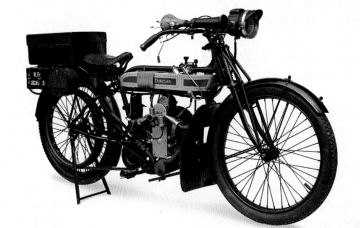

The Allies used about 20,000 of them during the War.

Ships and submarines

Ships of the First World War were built like great fortresses, with towering steel hulls and bristling with guns. They looked impregnable, but they faced a deadly threat from submarines that lurked beneath the waves.

HMS *Glorious* (UK)

Crew: 842   **Firepower:** 10 guns, 2 torpedo tubes
Launched: 1916   **Speed:** 32 knots (59kph/37mph)

With the guns of a battlecruiser, but the lightness and speed of a light cruiser, *Glorious* hunted down enemy ships in the North Sea. It was present at the surrender of the German High Seas Fleet in 1918.

After the War, *Glorious* was converted into an aircraft carrier, with a take-off and landing deck on top.

Lighter steel plating made the *Glorious* faster than many other ships.

HMS *Dreadnought* (UK)

Crew: 700-800

Launched: 1906

Firepower: 10 main guns, 27 smaller guns, 5 torpedo tubes

Speed: 21 knots (39kph/24mph)

The flag of the British Royal Navy was flown from the stern (rear).

Dreadnought was faster and had more firepower than any other battleship of its day. Its launch in 1906 led to an arms race between Germany and Britain, creating friction before the War broke out.

Dreadnought was armed with massive guns on its front and rear decks.

Dreadnought became the first and only battleship to sink a submarine, when it rammed a German U-boat on March 18, 1915.

Type U 31 submarine (Germany)

Crew: 35   **Firepower:** 6 torpedo tubes, 1 deck gun
Production: 1912-1915   **Speed:** 9.8 knots (18.1kph/11.3mph) submerged

Type U 31 was a medium-sized submarine, one of the most deadly and successful of the War. The U stands for *U boot* or *Unterseeboot*, meaning 'undersea boat' in German.

The German Imperial Navy flag was flown when above water.

Foudre (France)

Crew: 430 **Launched:** 1895

Firepower: 10 guns, 2 torpedo tubes, 4 seaplanes

Speed: 19 knots (35kph/22mph)

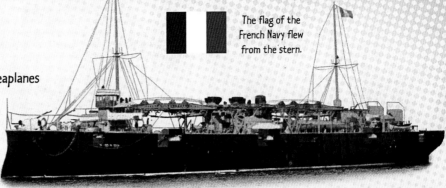

The flag of the French Navy flew from the stern.

A plane is lifted back on board *Foudre*.

Originally built to escort torpedo boats, *Foudre* was converted into the world's first aircraft carrier in 1911. It carried four seaplanes which could take off from the flat bow (front). The planes landed on water and were lifted back on board by crane.

SMS *Scharnhorst* (Germany)

Crew: 764

Launched: 1906

Firepower: 32 guns, 4 torpedo tubes

Speed: 22.7 knots (42kph/26mph)

Scharnhorst was part of the East Asia Squadron, based at the Chinese port of Tsingtao. In November 1914, it took part in a battle off Chile with the British Royal Navy.

Five weeks later, *Scharnhorst* and three other German ships were sunk near the Falkland Islands, losing 2,200 lives.

Rapid fire guns were fitted on the front deck.

Scharnhorst was armed with powerful guns along its sides and at the rear.

E-Class submarine (UK)

Crew: 30

Production: from 1912 to 1916

Firepower: 5 torpedo tubes, 1 deck gun

Speed: 10 knots (18.5kph/11.5mph)

58 E-Class subs were launched, becoming the most successful British submarines of the War. Three E-Class captains were awarded the Victoria Cross for bravery.

The British Royal Navy flag was flown when above water.

In 1914, submarine *E9* sank German cruiser *Hela*: the first Royal Navy submarine to sink a warship.

The Somme

On July 1, 1916, British and French commanders launched a massive attack against German forces near the River Somme in northwest France. Intended as a quick and decisive breakthrough, it turned out to be one of the longest, bloodiest and most futile battles in history.

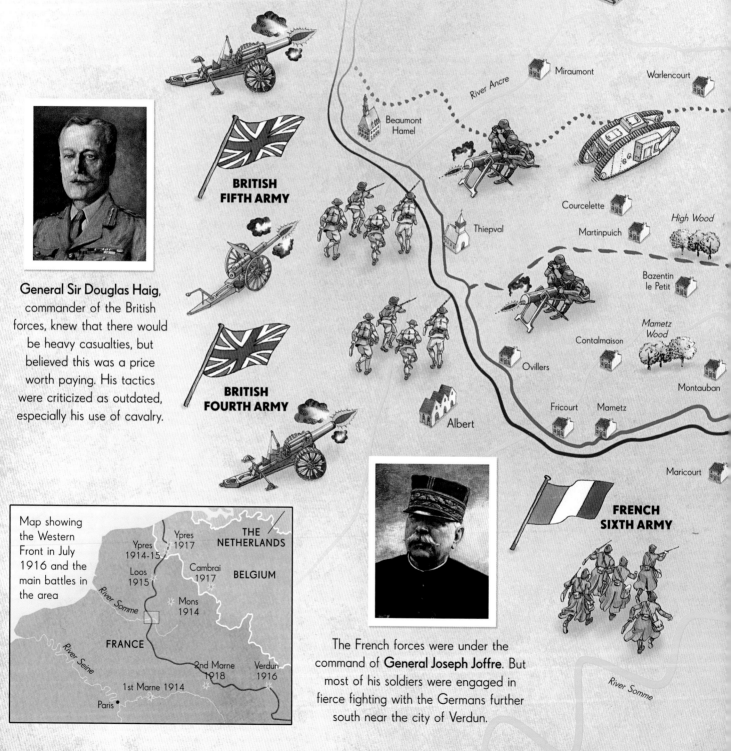

General Sir Douglas Haig, commander of the British forces, knew that there would be heavy casualties, but believed this was a price worth paying. His tactics were criticized as outdated, especially his use of cavalry.

BRITISH FIFTH ARMY

BRITISH FOURTH ARMY

FRENCH SIXTH ARMY

Miraumont
Warlencourt
River Ancre
Beaumont Hamel
Courcelette
High Wood
Thiepval
Martinpuich
Bazentin le Petit
Mametz Wood
Contalmaison
Ovillers
Montauban
Fricourt
Mametz
Albert
Maricourt
River Somme

Map showing the Western Front in July 1916 and the main battles in the area

THE NETHERLANDS
Ypres 1917
Ypres 1914-15
Loos 1915
Cambrai 1917
BELGIUM
Mons 1914
River Somme
FRANCE
2nd Marne 1918
Verdun 1916
1st Marne 1914
River Seine
Paris

The French forces were under the command of **General Joseph Joffre**. But most of his soldiers were engaged in fierce fighting with the Germans further south near the city of Verdun.

16

MAP GUIDE

———— Allied front line July 1, 1916

———— German front line July 1, 1916

– – – – German front line September 1, 1916

• • • • • German front line November 19, 1916

🏠 Town or village

🌳 Woodland

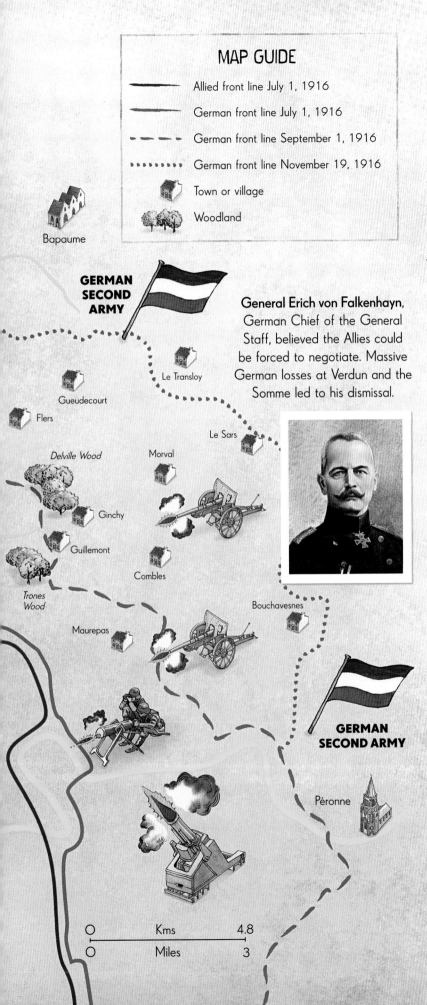

Bapaume

GERMAN SECOND ARMY

General Erich von Falkenhayn, German Chief of the General Staff, believed the Allies could be forced to negotiate. Massive German losses at Verdun and the Somme led to his dismissal.

Le Transloy

Gueudecourt

Flers

Le Sars

Delville Wood

Morval

Ginchy

Guillemont

Combles

Trones Wood

Maurepas

Bouchavesnes

GERMAN SECOND ARMY

Péronne

| O | Kms | 4.8 |
| O | Miles | 3 |

SOMME OFFENSIVE TIMELINE

June 24, 1916 3,000 Allied guns begin seven days of heavy bombardment against the German lines. But this fails to break the German positions.

Phase 1: July 1-14

July 1 About 100,000 British soldiers advance. 57,000 are cut down and nearly 21,000 killed. Elsewhere, French forces have more success.

Phase 2: July 14 - September 9

July 14 The British capture Bazentin Ridge, Mametz Wood and Contalmaison, but the Germans win them back.

August Some of the heaviest fighting takes place. German positions around the town of Thiepval are weakened by British attacks.

Phase 3: September 4-27

September 4 The French Tenth Army joins the French Sixth Army at the Somme.

September 15 Battle of Flers-Courcelette. British attack along a 16km (10 mile) front. Tanks (British Mark I) are used for the first time in battle.

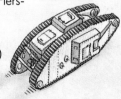

September 25 Thiepval finally falls to the Allies.

Phase 4: October - November 19

October Incessant rainfall turns the area into a muddy quagmire. Neither side is able to advance, and only small, localized attacks are possible.

Mid-November Battle of the Ancre. British capture Beaumont Hamel fort.

November 19 The Somme Offensive ends. After nearly six months of fighting and a total of 1.5 million casualties, the Allies have advanced just 8km (5 miles).

War art

Many artists joined up to fight, and painted and sculpted some of the horrors they had seen. But the British government also sent official war artists to record the devastation of the War.

Brass badge worn by soldiers of the Artists' Rifles

Gassed, by John Singer Sargent, painted in 1919

John Singer Sargent was the leading society painter of the day. In contrast to his usual work, *Gassed* shows the results of a mustard gas attack on British soldiers.

During a gas attack, soldiers had to wear masks to enable them to breathe.

The use of gas was one of the most terrifying developments of the War. Sargent's painting shows the suffering of the soldiers, many of whom have been burned and blinded by gas, as they are led shuffling towards the field hospital for treatment.

One of the first official British war artists, William Orpen painted some of the most disturbing images of the War. Here, the corpses of two German soldiers lie abandoned after the fighting has moved on elsewhere.

The Menin Road, by Paul Nash, painted in 1919

British artist Paul Nash enlisted, was invalided out after an accident, but returned to the Western Front in 1917 as an official war artist. This painting depicts a desolate landscape shattered by the fighting.

Dead Germans in a Trench, by William Orpen, painted in 1918

Nash's paintings capture the destruction of the War.

Stanley Spencer joined the Royal Army Medical Corps and was sent to Macedonia in the Balkans. This scene shows a stream of wounded soldiers brought to a field hospital after an attack.

Horses and donkeys were used to transport the wounded on stretchers from the battlefront to field hospitals.

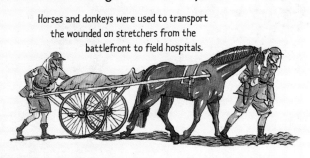

C.R.W. (Christopher) Nevinson joined an ambulance unit operating in northern France. This painting records his experiences there. A group of exhausted French soldiers stare blankly as they wait for their next orders.

Travoys Arriving with Wounded at a Dressing-Station at Smol, Macedonia, September 1916, by Stanley Spencer, painted in 1919

French Troops Resting, by C.R.W. Nevinson, painted in 1916

Die Skatspieler ('The Skat Players'),
by Otto Dix, painted in 1920

Otto Dix was a German artist who fought on both Fronts. His paintings depict the terrible scenes he witnessed. After the War, his work records his anger at the way many crippled soldiers were treated.

Back home, many injured war veterans were unable to work and were forced to beg.

L'Enfer ('Hell'), by Georges Leroux, painted in 1917-18

French artist Georges Leroux fought on the Western Front. This painting shows a group of terrified French soldiers taking shelter in a water-filled crater. All around is thick mud, barbed wire, broken weapons, smoke and exploding shells.

War leaders

Before the War, many of Europe's most powerful nations were headed by royal families who were related to each other and, in many cases, had been in power for centuries. By the end of the War, revolutions had swept most of them away.

Central Powers

Emperor Franz Josef I of Austria

Franz Josef I became emperor of Austria-Hungary in 1848. The assassination in 1914 of his heir, Archduke Franz Ferdinand, triggered a chain of events resulting in the outbreak of war. Franz Josef was succeeded by his great nephew Karl. He was overthrown in November 1918 and republics were declared in Austria and Hungary.

Franz Josef had a tragic personal life. His son killed himself, and his wife Elisabeth was assassinated in 1898.

Kaiser Wilhelm II of Germany

Grandson of British Queen Victoria, Wilhelm became Kaiser (ruler) of Germany in 1888. After dismissing his Chancellor, Bismarck, he adopted an aggressive foreign policy. After the War, he went into exile in the Netherlands, where he died in 1941.

Kaiser Wilhelm was fascinated by the military and liked to dress up in elaborate uniforms.

Helmet of the Prussian *Gardes du Corps*.

Sultan Mehmed V of Turkey

Becoming Sultan (ruler) of the Turkish Ottoman Empire in 1909, Mehmed had no real power, and declared war on the Allies on the advice of his ministers. He died just before the end of the War and was succeeded by his half-brother Mehmed VI. Turkey became a republic in 1922, ending 623 years of rule by the Ottoman dynasty.

Sultan Mehmed spent most of his life inside the Topkapi Palace in Constantinople (now Istanbul).

Allied Powers

King George V of Britain

King George, cousin to both Wilhelm II and Nicholas II, became king in 1910. His father Edward VII had signed the *Entente Cordiale* between Britain and France in 1904. His was almost the only monarchy to survive the War; George's granddaughter Elizabeth II is queen of Britain today.

Order of the Garter worn by George V in the painting on the left.

King Victor Emmanuel III of Italy

Victor Emmanuel III became King of Italy in 1900. Italy was neutral at the start of the War but, against the king's wishes, in 1915 entered on the side of the Allies. He ruled until 1946, when he was forced to abdicate and Italy became a republic.

President Poincaré with President Wilson at the Paris Peace Conference, 1919.

President Poincaré of France

Raymond Poincaré became Prime Minister of France in 1912, and was elected President the following year. With Prime Minister Georges Clemenceau, he hosted the 1919 Paris Peace Conference to end the War.

Tsar Nicholas II of Russia

One of the most tragic figures of the War, Tsar (or Emperor) Nicholas II abdicated during the Russian Revolution of 1917. In 1918, he and his wife and their children were murdered by the new communist rulers.

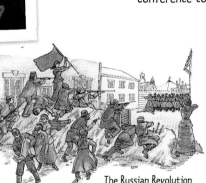

The Russian Revolution replaced the tsars with a communist Bolshevik government.

President Wilson of the USA

Thomas Woodrow Wilson was US President from 1913 to 1921. He was determined to keep the USA out of the War, but after months of German provocation, they joined the Allies in April 1917. Wilson was one of the founders of the League of Nations in 1919.

President Wilson was awarded the Nobel Peace Prize in 1919.

Famous people

The First World War inspired many acts of courage, cunning and determination from soldiers and civilians. Here are some of their amazing stories.

Edith Cavell

Edith Cavell was a British nurse in charge of a nursing school in Brussels, who helped more than 200 Allied soldiers escape from German-occupied Belgium. She was arrested and tried by the Germans, and was executed on October 12, 1915.

Edith Cavell's execution by firing squad caused uproar around the world.

Noel Chavasse

Captain Noel Chavasse, an army officer and doctor, was one of only three people ever to be awarded the Victoria Cross (Britain's top military medal) twice. First was in August 1916 when he cared for the wounded all day under heavy fire, and second was August 2, 1917, when he helped wounded soldiers although badly wounded himself. He died two days later and his gravestone was carved with two Victoria Crosses.

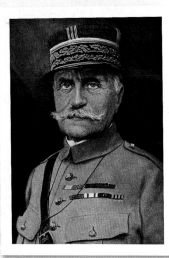

Marshal Foch

Ferdinand Foch was a French military leader, and hero of the 1914 Battle of the Marne, when the French succeeded in blocking the German advance on Paris. In 1918, he was made Commander-in-Chief of the Allied Armies and Marshal of the French army. On November 11, he accepted the German request for an armistice (ceasefire) at Compiègne in France.

The First Battle of the Marne was one of the most decisive battles of the War, leading to four years of trench warfare.

Paul von Lettow-Vorbeck

Paul von Lettow-Vorbeck commanded German forces in East Africa, attacking Allied forces there. The only German to invade British territory successfully during the entire War, he only surrendered his undefeated army after the Armistice was signed.

Lawrence of Arabia

One of the most glamorous figures of the War, T.E. (Thomas) Lawrence was a British intelligence officer and supporter of Arab independence from Turkish rule. After the War, he felt the Arab cause had been betrayed by the victorious European powers. He died in a motorcycle accident in 1935. His life story has become a legend.

The Red Baron

German Baron Manfred von Richthofen was the most successful air ace of the War, nicknamed the 'Red Baron' because of his red Fokker triplane. Believed to have shot down at least 80 enemy aircraft, he became famous all over Europe. In 1918, he was shot and fatally wounded while flying over France.

Mata Hari

Dutch-born dancer Margaretha Zelle is better known by her stage name, Mata Hari. Her contacts with German soldiers raised suspicions and in 1917 she was arrested in Paris, charged with spying and shot.

John Cornwell

John Cornwell, known as 'Jack', was a 16-year-old gunner on HMS Chester when the ship came under heavy fire at the Battle of Jutland. He remained at his post although fatally wounded, and was awarded the Victoria Cross for bravery.

Index

Usborne Quicklinks

For links to websites with video clips, games and activities to find out more about the First World War, go to the Usborne Quicklinks website at www.usborne.com/quicklinks and type in the title of the book.

The recommended websites are regularly reviewed and updated but, please note, Usborne Publishing is not responsible for the content of any website other than its own. We recommend that children are supervised while on the internet.

Acknowledgements

Cover: tr © National Geographic Image Collection / Alamy, tl akg-images / Interfoto, mr © Pictorial Press Ltd / Alamy, bl 7708-007 The Tank Museum; p2: ml Time & Life Picture / Getty Images, br Archives Charmet / The Bridgeman Art Library; p3: tr National Army Museum, London / The Bridgeman Art Library, bl © Mary Evans Picture Library / Alamy; p4: t © Pictorial Press Ltd / Alamy, ml © The Art Archive / Alamy, br De Agostini / Getty Images; p5: tr © Lordprice Collection / Alamy, ml Library of Congress, br IWM PST2763, bl IWM PST3283; p6: t © Darren Harbar Photography courtesy of The Shuttleworth Collection, b © Rob Walls / Alamy; p7: tl © James Nesterwitz / Alamy, mr National Museum of the U.S. Air Force photo, ml © Detail Heritage / Alamy, br Courtesy of Museum of Flight, Seattle, photo by CIAR; p8: tr IWM Q66838, m IWM Q58467, bl IWM Q65970; p9: tr IWM Q67219, ml IWM Q105405, br National Museum of the U.S. Air Force photo; p10: tl 1195-A1 The Tank Museum, br 8931-A2 The Tank Museum; p11: tl 7708-002 The Tank Museum, mr 7708-007 The Tank Museum, ml © Paris – Musée de l'Armée, Dist. RMN-Grand Palais / Emilie Cambier, br © Paris – Musée de l'Armée, Dist. RMN-Grand Palais / Marie Bruggeman; p12: t © akg-images / ullstein bild, b IWM 4107-005-1; p13: tr IWM Q15077, ml Civico Museo di Guerra per la pace Diego de Henriquez C.T. 6030, mr IWM Q14510, bl Courtesy of Chris Roberts, The Great War Society; p14: tr IWM SP3092, ml IWM Q38712; p15: tr © Walker Naval Archive, m IWM Q80706; p16: tl © Photos 12 / Alamy, b © The Art Archive / Alamy; p17: m © The Art Archive / Alamy; p18: t IWM ART1460, br IWM ART2242, bl IWM ART2955; p19: tr IWM ART2268, ml IWM ART5219 © Nevinson / Bridgeman 2013, mr The Art Archive / Private Collection / Gianni Dagli Orti, © DACS 2016; p20: tr © Lebrecht Music and Arts Photo Library / Alamy, ml IBL Collections / Mary Evans, mr akg-images / Interfoto, br Mary Evans / Grenville Collins Postcard Collection; p21: tl © Prisma Bildagentur AG / Alamy, tr © Imagestate Media Partners Limited – Impact Photos / Alamy, mr © Interfoto / Alamy, ml Château de Versailles, France / Giraudon / The Bridgeman Art Library, br © The Print Collector / Corbis, bl © Everett Collection Historical / Alamy; p22: tl © Raymond Lynde, Nurse Edith Cavell, undated, oil on canvas, Norfolk Museums Service (Norwich Castle Museum & Art Gallery), mr © PA / PA Archive/Press Association Images, bl © ITPix / Alamy; p23: tl © The Art Archive / Alamy, tr IWM ART2473, ml © GL Archive / Alamy, br © Mary Evans Picture Library, bl IWM Q20883

IWM = Courtesy of the Trustees of Imperial War Museums

With thanks to Ruth King

Additional illustration by Giovanni Paulli   Digital manipulation by John Russell

This edition first published in 2017 by Usborne Publishing Ltd., Usborne House, 83-85 Saffron Hill, London EC1N 8RT, England. www.usborne.com Copyright © 2017, 2016, 2015, 2014 Usborne Publishing Ltd.